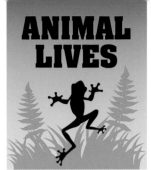

ANIMAL LIVES

AMAZING ANIMALS
STICKER ACTIVITY BOOK

by Lynn Huggins-Cooper

Silver Dolphin

San Diego, California

Silver Dolphin Books
An imprint of the
Baker & Taylor Publishing Group
10350 Barnes Canyon Road
San Diego, CA 92121
www.silverdolphinbooks.com

ISBN-13: 978-1-60710-138-3
ISBN-10: 1-60710-138-6

Made in China.

Created by Walter Foster Publishing, Inc.
Concept Development by Pauline Foster
and Heidi Kellenberger
Guidebook written by Lynn Huggins-
Cooper
Activity cards written by Gary Koltookian
Project Management by Rebecca Razo
Edited by Rebecca Razo and Sandy Phan
Art Direction by Shelley Baugh
Production Design by Debbie Aiken,
Rae Siebels, and Wendy Vandenborck
Production Management by Irene
Chan, Lawrence Marquez, and Nicole
Szawlowski

1 2 3 4 5 14 13 12 11 10

Photo Credits: Key: t = top, b = bottom, c = center, l = left,
m = middle, r = right, FC = front cover, BC = back cover
A = Alamy, BSP = BigStockPhoto.com, C = Corbis,
D = Dreamstime.com, F = Fotolibra.com, G = Getty Images,
ISP = iStockphoto.com, M = Morguefile.com, N = Nature
Picture Library (naturepl.com), P = Photolibrary,
PS = Photoshot, S = Shutterstock.com, SDB = Starry Dog
Books, SPL = Science Photo Library.

Crazy Creatures: © 5 S/ © Markross 6t D/ © Twwphoto
6b P/ © Daniel Cox 7D/ © Alisongoff 8t G/ © Tim Laman
8b F/ © David Knowles 9 G/ © Roine Magnusson 10t/
© Dr. Rafe M. Brown 10b P/ © Wells Bert & Babs 11 C/ ©
Gary Bell/zefa 12 D/ © Jolka 100; 13t S/ © Dino 13b C/ ©
Saed Hindash/Star Ledger 14t SPL/ © Rod Planck 14b C/ ©
Nigel J. Dennis/Gallo Images 15 C/ © Gavriel Jecan 16 C/
© Hans Reinhard/zefa 16b SPL/ © Nicholas Smythe 17 P/
© 18t S/ © David M. Dennis 18b C/ © Markus Botzek/zefa
19 S/ © Patsy A. Jacks 22m S/ © Michael Lynch 22b ISP/
© Holger Mette 23 P/ © clearviewstock.com 24b P/ © M
Delpho 25b S/ © Stan Osolinski 25t S/ © Vova Pomortzeff
26t C/ © Wolfgang Thieme/dpa 26b ISP/ © James Richey
27 ISP/ © Elzbieta Sekowska 28t ISP/ © Anna Yu 28-29 C/
© 29t S/ © Timothy G. Laman 30 P/ © Michael DeYoung
31 C/ © Harald Bolten 32t C/ © Bruce Robinson 32b C/
© Bruce Robinson 33 A **Revolting Reptiles:** © 34-35 S/
© Snowleopard l 36t ISP/ © Klaus Nilkens 36b S/ © Dr.
Morely Reed 37 S/ © Snowleopard l 38m G/ © Claus
Meyer 38b/ © Wikipedia 39 G/ © Pete Oxford 40t S/ ©
40b S/ © Arthur Morris 41 A/ © Juniors Bildarchiv 42t
PS/ © 42b S/ © Michael & Patricia Fogden 43 ISP/ © Kris
Hanke 44 C/ © Joe McDonald 45t ISP/ © Bob Kupbens
45b G/ © Mark Moffett 46b S/ © Snowleopard l 46-47 C/
© Wolfgang Thieme/dpa 47b SP/ © Paul Zahl 48t C/ ©
Joe McDonald 48b C/ © Theo Allofs 49 ISP/ © Norman
Bateman 52t G/ © Pete Oxford 52b P/ © Joe McDonald 53
G/ © Mike Severns 54t C/ ©Michael & Patricia Fogden 54b
ISP/ © Tillsonburg 55 C/ ©Theo Allofs/zefa 56-57 C/ ©
Frans Lanting 57t ISP/ © Timothy Martin 57b PS/ © Kevin
Schafer/NHPA 58b P/ ©Zigmund Leszczynski 59 A/ © Mark
Bowler Amazon-Images 60bl PS/ © Ken Griffiths/NHPA
60-61 S/ © John Bell 61b C/ © Phillipe Psaila 62m C/ ©
Michael & Patricia Fogden 62b SP/ © Joe McDonald 63 C
Beastly Birds, Bats & Bugs: © 64-65 S/ © Arlene Jean Gee
66t C/ © Craig Aurness 66b S/ © iDesign 67 S/ © Phillip
Date 68t ISP/ © Marshall Bruce 68b C/ © Joe McDonald 71
ISP/ © Susan Flashman 72 N/ © Art Segal 73t S/ © Michael
Ransburg 73b ISP/ © Diego Cervo 74b M/ © sillypieces
74-75 G/ © Roine Magnussen 75b C/ © Roger Tidman 76t
P/ © Juniors Bildarchiv 76b S/ © Rudolph Kotulan 77 S/
© Andy Z 78 ISP/ © David T. Gomez 78-79 ISP/ © Paul
Tessier 79tr C/ © Michael & Patricia Fogden 82t C/ © Gary
Bell/zefa 82b S/ © Lori Froeb 83 ISP/ © Mark Higgins 84t
F/ © Linda Wright 84b P/ © Friedemann Koster 85 G/
© Roger Powell/Foto Natura 86m C/ © Kit Kittle 86bl D/
© Argument 86-87 G/ © Eric Rorer 87 C/ © Hans Dieter
Brandl/Frank Lane Picture Agency 88t C/ © W Perry Conway
88b C/ © Prof. Phil Myers 89 C/ © Gary Braasch 90t P/
© Dr. John P. Dumbacher 90b P/ © Juniors Bildarchiv 91
SDB/ © Katherine Haluska 92t BSP/ © Stuart Elflett 92b D/
© Pixelman 93 D

CONTENTS

Words in **bold** are explained in the glossary on pages
94–96. Answers to questions appear upside down at the
bottom of the page.

How to Use This Book

Each chapter in this book focuses on a different animal, providing fascinating facts and teaching you all you ever wanted to know about these amazing creatures. But that's not all—this book also contains more than 200 stickers and 24 activity cards, so the fun doesn't have to end when you're finished reading!

In each chapter is a background you can use to create your own scene with the animal stickers on pages 97–101. You can make a scene with all crazy creatures, all revolting reptiles, or all beastly birds, bats, and bugs, or you can mix it up and let all the animals roam together. You'll also find pages in each chapter that include "missing" images—find the correct stickers on page 103 and place them on the pages to complete each scene. To answer the questions throughout the book, use the stickers on page 105. Then you'll find more stickers for endless animal fun.

At the back of the book you'll find 24 punch-out activity cards filled with fun facts, jokes, games, and other great ways to keep learning about your favorite animals. All the cards are two-sided—some have different activities on each side and others have one activity that requires you to turn the card over for the answer. Let's start learning!

CHAPTER 1:
CRAZY CREATURES

Really wild!

The animal world is full of amazing creatures. Some look cute, but the sweetest-looking animals may be very fierce. Creatures that look scary may be gentle and shy. Other animals are colorful and extraordinary looking, which helps them survive in their natural environment.

Weasels are fierce predators. They have beautiful fur like a cat, but you cannot stroke them!

Turn to page 103 to find the sticker that completes this scene.

Bad behavior?

Animals kill other animals because they need to eat. Sometimes, animals attack people, and we think of this behavior as vicious. All wild animals can be dangerous. If a human enters a bear's **territory,** the bear may follow its instincts and attack, just as it would if any other wild animal threatened its territory. Its behavior is not vicious, it is natural wild animal behavior.

Bears will attack if they are surprised, feel threatened, or are protecting their territory or *cubs*.

Leafy sea dragons are a type of fish. They are related to the sea horse. Their leafy *appendages* may look strange, but they help sea dragons hide among floating seaweed.

QUESTION

The weasel has fur that feels similar to which domestic house pet?

Answer: Cat (see page 6)

Smelly animals

Some animals really stink! However, the smells have a purpose. A stinky smell can make an animal more attractive to its mate, or it may keep predators at a safe distance.

Moonrats have a long, sensitive nose for detecting smells. They hiss at other moonrats in their territory.

Moonrats

Moonrats live in the rain forests and **mangrove swamps** of Sumatra, Borneo, and the Malay Peninsula. They mark their **dens** with a liquid that smells like rotting onions or garlic. The smell warns other moonrats and predators to stay away from their territories.

Polecats mostly hunt at night. Their keen sense of smell helps them detect rabbits, rats, birds, snakes, frogs, and fish.

Turn to page 103 to find the sticker that completes this scene.

Polecats

Polecats live in woodland areas of Europe, Asia, and North Africa. They mark their territories with a foul-smelling liquid, made in **glands** at the base of the tail. People once used the word "polecat" to describe someone with a character as foul as the polecat's smell.

In the early 1900s, musk oxen were hunted nearly to *extinction* for their meat and hide. Now, however, they are protected by law.

Musk ox

The musk ox lives in cold regions in Greenland and northern Canada. Males, called bulls, produce a strong-smelling liquid in glands just under their eyes. To release the smell, the bull rubs its face on trees and bushes. The smell attracts females, who can detect it from a long way off.

The musk ox has long hair with a thick layer of wool underneath.

Animal stickers

Some animals are sticky and others can stick to things using **suction**. Long, sticky tongues allow some animals to catch their food. Others use suction pads to move around or cling onto branches or rocks.

When alarmed by a predator, the black-spotted sticky frog puffs itself up and turns its back to the predator, showing off two large spots. To the predator, this view looks like a snake's head.

Black-spotted sticky frog

The black-spotted sticky frog lives in the rain forests of Southeast Asia. At night, it hunts for insects on the forest floor. The frog releases a sticky slime when it is threatened, making it an unpleasant meal for predators.

The numbat eats about 20,000 termites every day.

Numbat

The numbat, or banded anteater, lives in the forests of southwest Australia. It uses its nose to track down **termite mounds**. When it finds one, the numbat pokes its long, sticky tongue into holes in the mound. The termites stick to the tongue and the numbat has a feast!

Crown-of-thorns starfish

The crown-of-thorns starfish lives in warm seas and feeds on coral. Thousands of tiny tube feet underneath its arms help the starfish move around. The feet have suction cups that allow the starfish to cling onto rocks.

The crown-of-thorns starfish is covered in long, poisonous spines.

Disease carriers

Many animals carry diseases that can be passed on to each other, such as **mange** in dogs. Some animals carry diseases that can be passed on to humans, too.

It is important to wash your hands after playing with your dog or cat so that you don't pick up any diseases.

Dogs and cats

Dogs and cats carry **parasites**, such as **tapeworms** and **roundworms,** that live inside them. The eggs of the parasites pass out in the **feces** of the dog or cat. People can end up with these parasites, too, if they get the eggs on their hands by touching dogs and then eating without washing their hands. Regularly **"worming,"** or treating, your dog or cat kills the worms.

Be careful not to hold pigeons if you feed them, as this carries a health risk.

ANIMAL FACT

In the 16th century, pigeon feces was used to make gunpowder; it was considered to be valuable!

Pigeons

Many towns around the world have large numbers of pigeons. The birds can carry a disease that affects their lungs and the lungs of people. Symptoms of the disease are mild in pigeons, but can be serious in humans. People catch the disease by breathing in dust containing specks of the birds' feces. **Bacteria** in the feces can give a person a fever.

Turn to page 103 to find the sticker that completes this scene.

Rats

Rats are **rodents** that live where people do. They spread many diseases, including food poisoning, **typhus,** and **bubonic plague.** In the 14th century, the plague became known as the Black Death. It was passed on to humans by infected fleas from the rats. The Black Death may have killed as many as 50 million people in Europe.

Rats eat the food in our trash. Many live near us, in the *sewers* beneath the streets.

Nasty noses

Some animals have amazing noses that they use to seek out food. They may smell their **prey** from a long way off, or use their sensitive noses to detect movements made by their prey.

The star-nosed mole's tentacles help it to identify prey by touch because it is blind.

Star-nosed mole

The star-nosed mole of North America looks like an ordinary mole—except for its nose: 22 fleshy tentacles stick out from the nose and wriggle constantly. They help the mole feel movements in the ground made by its prey, such as worms.

Aardvark

The aardvark lives in Africa in the area south of the Sahara Desert. It has a long **snout,** which it uses to sniff out its food—ants and termites—as it walks along at night. It may walk as far as 18 miles in one night, pressing its nose to the ground to pick up their scent. It also listens for any sound of movement made by the termites.

When an aardvark digs a burrow or breaks into a termite mound, it can squeeze its nostrils shut to keep out the dust.

The nose of the male proboscis monkey can be up to 5.5 inches long. It makes the monkey's warning calls louder.

ANIMAL FACT

A male proboscis monkey pushes its nose out of the way when it eats!

Proboscis monkey

The proboscis monkey is named after the large, wobbly nose, or proboscis, of the male monkey. It is thought that the large nose helps the male attract a mate. It lives in the swampy mangrove forests of Borneo and wades through the water on its back legs. This makes it very unusual, as most monkeys move around using all four legs.

QUESTION

Which sea creature can grow to be as big as a car tire?

Answer: Crown-of-thorns starfish (see page 11)

Poisonous animals

The duck-billed platypus has a flat bill like a duck's beak, a furry body, and strong limbs that help it swim and dig.

There are many poisonous creatures around the world. Some animals use **venom** for defense. Others use it to catch larger prey.

Duck-billed platypus

The duck-billed platypus lives in eastern Australia. It eats frogs, fish, and insects. The male platypus has a **spur** on each of its back legs that holds a strong poison. If threatened, the platypus stabs its attacker with a spur and injects the poison. The poison is strong enough to kill a dog.

Turn to page 103 to find the sticker that completes this scene.

Solenodons

The two **species** of solenodons are both **endangered.** They live on the Caribbean islands of Hispaniola and Cuba. When a solenodon attacks its prey, such as a spider, poisonous **saliva** flows into its victim along grooves in its lower front teeth. The poison stuns the prey, making it easier to grasp.

Pit vipers

The diamondback rattlesnake is a type of pit viper that is common in North and Central America. Pit vipers are venomous snakes. They can sense body heat, which enables them to sneak up on their prey at night. They bite to kill, but will also bite in self-defense. Their hollow fangs inject poison into their prey.

Here, a diamondback rattlesnake is having its venom removed. The venom is used to make antivenin, a medicine used to treat snakebites.

Vicious animals

The weasel's long, slender body allows it to follow its prey into small burrows.

Animals such as killer whales, tigers, and bears are well-known for being fierce; however, the world is also full of small, vicious creatures that hunt their prey aggressively.

Northern short-tailed shrew

The northern short-tailed shrew is small—but very fierce! It needs to eat three times its body weight each day, so it spends its time hunting for insects, spiders, worms, and snails.

Weasels

Weasels live mainly in the **Northern Hemisphere.** The weasel is a savage hunter. Weasels prey on mice, voles, frogs, birds, and rabbits. They eat eggs, too! When excited, weasels do a strange, hopping war dance. Some **biologists** believe they perform the dance to confuse their prey.

Both northern and southern short-tailed shrews live in North America. They use a special *toxin* to paralyze larger prey.

Tasmanian devil

The Tasmanian devil looks like a small bear and is very vicious. It uses its powerful jaws to crack bones and tear fur and flesh. In addition to feeding on **carrion**, or animals that are already dead, it also eats the **larvae** of some types of beetles, and it attacks poultry.

The Tasmanian devil was named "devil" because of the high-pitched screeching noises it makes at night. When threatened, it opens its mouth in a yawn, which looks aggressive but is really a sign of fear.

QUESTION

What is the name of the poison that pit vipers inject into their prey with their fangs?

Answer:
Venom
(see page 17)

ANIMAL FACT

Various words are used to describe a group of weasels, including a gang, pack, confusion, and boogle!

Create a scene

Use the stickers on page 97
to create your own amazing animal habitat!

Sneaky animals

Some animals use sneaky methods to catch their prey or to escape from predators. They may use disguises, move quietly, or use clever tricks.

The vampire bat quietly creeps along the ground as it approaches its prey, such as a cow or a pig.

Vampire bats

Vampire bats are found in Africa and South America. The common vampire bat is able to walk, jump, and hop. This means it can creep up to its prey and hop onto its body. As it bites, the bat's saliva enters the wound and makes the animal's skin go numb. The animal does not know it has been bitten.

Turn to page 103 to find the sticker that completes this scene.

Tarsiers

Tarsiers are related to monkeys and lemurs. They are found on islands in Southeast Asia. Tarsiers have good eyesight and hunt mostly at night. They jump onto their prey, including insects, birds, and snakes. They pounce and grab the animal with their paws.

Tarsiers have large pads at the end of their long fingers to help grip branches and prey tightly.

Raccoons

Raccoons are very sneaky. Their specially **adapted** paws can open latches and doors. Their black eye patches make them look like masked bandits—and they can act like them, too! They often steal food from houses, cars, and campsites.

Raccoons often rifle through trash bins in search of food.

ANIMAL FACT

Many people think of raccoons as pests because the animals spill the trash from bins in the neighborhood.

Terrifying tongues

Some animals have amazing tongues. They may be forked, sticky, or just incredibly long. Tongues can be used for digging insects from the ground or grabbing leaves and branches.

The okapi's tongue is 14 inches long. It is as sensitive and flexible as a human hand.

Okapi

The okapi is brown with a striped **rump** and legs. It is related to the giraffe. A shy animal, it lives in the dense forests of the African Congo and was only discovered in 1901. The okapi uses its long, black tongue to grab leaves and branches and pull them into its mouth.

QUESTION

Which animal always looks like it is wearing a mask?

Answer: Raccoon (see page 23)

The sun bear's slithery tongue is up to 10 inches long.

Sun bear

The sun bear lives in the forests of Southeast Asia. It likes to make its home high up in the branches of trees. The sun bear sleeps or sunbathes by day and hunts at night. It has long, curved claws that it uses to dig for insects. It also pokes its long tongue into holes in rotten wood to catch insects or lick up honey.

Echidnas

Echidnas, or spiny anteaters, live in Australia, Tasmania, and New Guinea. They have small nostrils and a tiny mouth at the end of their long, tubelike beaks. They eat ants and termites, which they catch with their long, sticky tongue.

ANIMAL FACT

If grabbed by the back of the neck, the sun bear can swivel its head around inside its loose neck skin to bite its attacker.

An echidna hunts by poking its nose into the ground, leaving behind cone-shaped nose prints.

TRUE OR FALSE?

The word "boogle" is used to describe a group of weasels.

Answer: True! (see page 19)

Ugly brutes

Some animals look ugly. They may have no hair, have lumps on their faces, or be large and flabby with big noses. Although they look strange, these features are special adaptations that help these animals survive.

Turn to page 103 to find the sticker that completes this scene.

These naked mole rats are coming out of a tunnel in a zoo. Their small eyes and ears are almost hidden in the folds of their skin.

Naked mole rat

The naked mole rat lives in long tunnels in the grassy regions of eastern Africa. It lives in groups of 20 to 300 members, ruled over by a queen. Hairless skin prevents the mole rat from overheating in its underground home.

Adult male elephant seals have a large, fleshy nose used for making roaring noises during the mating season.

Elephant seals

Elephant seals are huge creatures with folds of fat and skin that make them look rumpled and creased. Their thick layer of fat is called blubber. It keeps them warm when they dive into the icy ocean to search for food.

Warthog

The warthog belongs to the pig family. It lives in Africa. The male warthog has four hard bumps on its face that look like warts, which is how it got its name. Males and females have curved tusks growing out of their mouths, which they use as weapons.

ANIMAL FACT

A warthog's canine teeth grow constantly. It uses them to dig and search for food.

The four hard bumps on the warthog's face cushion the blows when it fights.

Gross eaters

Some animals have unpleasant eating habits. They may feast on dead animals, digest the bones of their prey in acid, or use their strong jaws to rip their prey apart.

The wolverine's sharp, powerful claws help it kill prey.

Wolverine

The wolverine is sometimes called a skunk bear or glutton. It lives in Alaska, Siberia, northern Canada, and Scandinavia. It often eats the remains of animals killed by wolves. It will also kill prey by pouncing on an animal from a tree or rock.

ANIMAL FACT

Hyenas have strong acid in their stomach. This helps them digest chunks of meat and bones.

Hyenas

The spotted hyena uses its large jaws to crush the bones of its prey and tear through thick skin.

Hyenas are strong, doglike creatures that live in Africa and India. Although they **scavenge** and eat carrion (dead animals), they also catch young hippos, gazelles, zebras, wildebeests, and antelopes. The stomach of a spotted hyena can hold up to 33 pounds of meat, so it can go for several days without food.

QUESTION

Which type of cat marks its territory with a foul-smelling liquid?

Pangolins

Pangolins are also called scaly anteaters. They live in tropical Asia and Africa, and are covered with brown scales. The pangolin eats termites, ants, and other insects, which it sniffs out and catches on its long, sticky tongue. It has no teeth. Instead, horny plates in its stomach grind down the food before it is digested.

Scary beasts

There are frightening myths and superstitions about some animals, but these stories are not true! It is important to learn about these amazing animals.

Wolves

Wolves live in many northern countries. Gray wolves are fast runners and chase down their prey. They hunt deer, elk, moose, hares, and beavers. In some places, wolves kill farm animals and eat trash from bins. Wolves live in packs of up to 20. These packs are very close and organized; they travel, hunt, and raise families together.

Wolves have large, sharp teeth that help to tear meat.

The aye-aye's *habitat* is the tropical forest. It hunts at night in the trees.

ANIMAL FACT

Some people in Madagascar believe that a person will die if an aye-aye points its long middle finger at them.

Aye-aye

The aye-aye lives in the rain forests of Madagascar. Using its long, bony middle finger, it taps on tree branches and listens for beetles and grubs moving under the bark. When it hears a grub, it picks it out of the bark using its long finger. It also uses its middle finger to scoop out the flesh from inside coconuts.

Answer: Giraffe (see page 24)

QUESTION

The okapi is related to what animal?

Terrors of the deep

The ocean is home to some very strange fish. Some have terrifying teeth. Others have small, light-producing cells on their bodies that attract prey.

Spookfish

Some types of spookfish are also known as barreleyes because they have tube-shaped eyes. Barreleyes live deep in the Atlantic, Pacific, and Indian oceans, at depths of 1,300 to 8,000 feet. Their sensitive eyes point upward and are able to detect **predators** swimming in the dim water above them.

At night, marine hatchetfish rise to a depth of 150 feet below the surface to feed. They return to deeper water before dawn.

Marine hatchetfish

Marine hatchetfish live at depths of 600 to 20,000 feet in the Atlantic, Pacific, and Indian oceans. Small cells called photophores located on the undersides of their bodies give off tiny spots of light that point downward. These lights may attract mates. They may also lure prey from below.

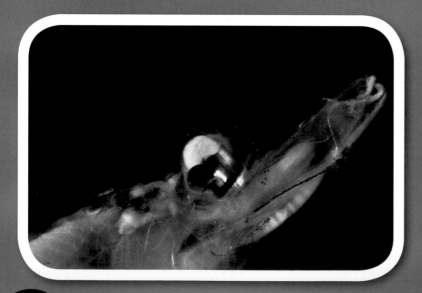

The bones of a barreleye's skull are so thin that you can see its brain between its eyes.

Barbeled dragonfish

Barbeled dragonfish live in tropical oceans at depths of up to 5,000 feet. The female has a long barbel under its lower jaw that it waves backward and forward to attract prey. The barbel has a light-producing organ at the tip, and the fish can flash the light on and off. As soon as prey draws near, the dragonfish snaps it up with its ferocious jaws.

The barbeled dragonfish is a fierce predator in spite of its small size—it is about 6 inches long.

QUESTION

The numbat eats up to 20,000 of what a day?

Answer: Termites (see page 10)

ANIMAL FACT

The young of some dragonfish have eyes on the end of long stalks, unlike their parents.

CHAPTER 2:
REVOLTING REPTILES

Cold blood!

Reptiles include lizards, snakes, and crocodiles. **Amphibians** include soft-skinned frogs and salamanders. Both amphibians and reptiles are cold-blooded animals, which means that their body temperatures are the same as the temperature of the surrounding air.

Many salamanders, such as the Ecuador mushroomtongue salamander, do not have lungs or *gills*. They get the oxygen they need through their skin.

Like modern crocodiles, the dinosaur T. rex had sharp teeth for grabbing food.

Reptiles old and new

Dinosaurs were reptiles that lived millions of years ago. Like modern reptiles, they had no fur and they hatched from eggs. The teeth and skin of some dinosaurs were similar to those of modern alligators, and some dinosaurs may have been as intelligent as crocodiles. Dinosaurs are now extinct.

Amphibians

Amphibians have adapted to life in and out of water. They are able to breathe through their skin, although most adult amphibians also have lungs for breathing. When they face a predator, many amphibians pretend to be dead in hopes that the predator will leave them alone. Some amphibians produce toxins in their skin that make them taste bad to predators.

Poison dart frogs have toxic skin. Local tribespeople in South America rub the frogs against the skin of young parrots. The poison makes the parrots grow feathers of different colors.

Funky frogs

Frogs live all over the world, except in icy **Antarctica.** Most species live in tropical countries with warm, damp climates, but some prefer hot deserts. Some frogs have developed unusual ways of protecting their young.

Turn to page 103 to find the sticker that completes this scene.

Paradox frog

The paradox frog lives in ponds and lakes in South America and on the Caribbean island of Trinidad. Adult paradox frogs are about 2 inches long, but their **tadpoles** are much larger—up to 9 inches long. Tadpoles shrink as they develop into adults.

The paradox frog makes a grunting noise like a pig. It digs in the muddy bottoms of ponds to find insects and larvae to eat.

Pouched frog

The pouched frog lives in a small area of eastern Australia. The female lays a pile of eggs in damp soil rather than in water. As the eggs hatch into tiny white tadpoles, the male hops into the middle of the pile, and the tadpoles wriggle into two pouches just above his back legs. The tadpoles stay in his pouches until they are ready to emerge as fully formed small frogs.

This frog is not shown life-size here. At only 1 inch long, the pouched frog is about the size of a cherry.

ANIMAL FACT

Sometimes Lake Titicaca frogs are eaten in restaurants in Bolivia and Peru.

The Lake Titicaca frog can survive underwater, as it absorbs oxygen from the water through its skin. It sometimes does strange "push-ups" underwater that disturb the water and make more oxygen flow.

Lake Titicaca frog

The Lake Titicaca frog lives only in Lake Titicaca in South America. Lake Titicaca is 12,500 feet above sea level. At this **altitude,** the air is very thin—it has less oxygen than places nearer sea level. To cope with these conditions, the Lake Titicaca frog has developed saggy skin with many folds. The frog soaks up oxygen through its skin, and the extra skin increases the amount of oxygen that it can absorb.

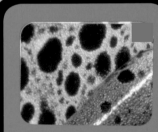

QUESTION

What part of the poison dart frog is poisonous?

Answer: Its skin (see page 37)

Beastly biters

Alligators, crocodiles, and gharials have lots of terrifying teeth. They grow replacements if their teeth are lost or broken.

Alligators

There are two species of alligators—the huge American alligator and the much smaller Chinese alligator, which is almost extinct. Alligators live in swamps, freshwater ponds, rivers, and wetlands. They pounce on their prey, including reptiles, **mammals,** and birds, if the prey gets too close.

The male gharial has a small growth on the end of its snout. It uses this to make a humming noise that warns other males to stay away, as well as to blow bubbles that attract females.

Gharials

The gharial lives in small numbers in the rivers of northeast India, Bangladesh, Nepal, and Bhutan. Large males can reach almost 20 feet long. The gharial is clumsy on land, but is very quick in the water. It catches small fish and other creatures by snapping its jaws as it sweeps its head from side to side.

Alligators have a tendency to overheat after activity; they often lie in water to cool down.

Caimans

Caimans are the largest predators in South America's **Amazon basin.** They can reach 13 to 16 feet long—the length of an average SUV. Caimans eat fish like piranhas, which are also aggressive meat eaters. Caimans also eat turtles, birds, deer, **tapirs,** and even **anacondas.**

An adult caiman swallows a large fish whole. The acid in the caiman's stomach is so strong that it can digest every part of its prey, including bones and tough skin.

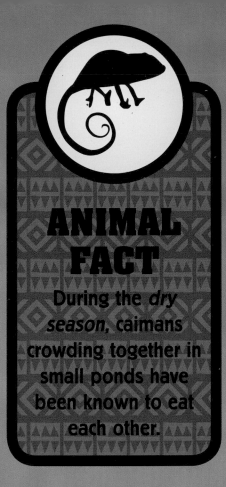

ANIMAL FACT

During the *dry season*, caimans crowding together in small ponds have been known to eat each other.

QUESTION

Which amphibian is found in every region of the world except Antarctica?

Answer: Frog (see page 38)

41

Nasty noises

Some reptiles and amphibians make creepy noises that can be very loud. Some let out strange screams. Some imitate the noises made by other animals.

A male midwife toad will carry eggs on its back legs until they hatch.

Midwife toads

Midwife toads live in northern Africa and parts of Europe. The males make a noise that sounds like an electronic beep. The females lay strings of eggs, which the males stick to their legs using slime. When the eggs are ready to hatch into tadpoles, the males wade into the water so the tadpoles can swim off.

Smoky frog

The smoky frog, or smoky jungle frog, lives mainly in tropical rain forests in Central and South America. If attacked, the smoky frog makes a high-pitched scream.

The smoky frog will eat small birds, mammals, and even snakes that are twice its size.

Unlike many frogs, coqui frogs do not have webbed feet. They have disks or pads on their toes that help them grip onto plants.

Coqui frogs

The name of these frogs is pronounced "co-KEE," which sounds like the noise they make. Coqui frogs originally lived on several Caribbean islands, but they are also found in huge numbers on the Hawaiian Islands. They reached Hawaii by accidentally hopping aboard cargo ships.

TRUE OR FALSE?

A caiman can grow to be 13 to 16 feet long.

ANIMAL FACT

Coqui frogs make a noise that measures 90 to 100 *decibels* 1.5 feet away from the frog, which is the equivalent of a speeding train.

Answer: True! (see page 41)

Poisonous pests

Some reptiles and amphibians are poisonous. They might have poison in their skin, their saliva, or their venomous fangs.

The horned viper has two long scales on its head that look like horns. The horns may help protect the snake's eyes and may make the snake harder for predators to spot.

Horned viper

The horned viper lives in northern Africa and parts of the Middle East. When hunting, it digs its body into the sand and lies in wait. The only parts of the snake that remain visible are its horns. When prey approaches, it lurches out of the sand and strikes, shooting poison from its fangs. The horned viper preys on unwary rodents, small snakes, lizards, and birds.

QUESTION
What type of frog does not have webbed feet?

Answer: Coquí frog (see page 43)

The Gila monster has powerful claws for digging burrows, but kills with poisonous saliva.

Gila monster

The Gila monster is a lizard. It kills and eats birds, rodents, and other lizards by biting them and then chewing until venomous saliva flows into the wound. The Gila monster lives in the southwest United States and northern Mexico. Its teeth are loose and if a few get broken, it just grows some more.

Poison dart frogs

Poison dart frogs are found in Central and South America. Most are brightly colored to warn predators that they are dangerous to eat. They **secrete,** or release, poison through their skin.

The most toxic poison dart frog is the golden poison frog, which carries enough poison to kill as many as 10 humans.

Sneaky salamanders

Many salamander species are known for having a sneaky trick. If a predator grabs the salamander by the tail, part of the tail breaks off and wriggles around like a separate creature. This distracts the predator, so the salamander can run away unharmed.

Fire salamander

The fire salamander lives in the forests of southern and central Europe. It hunts mainly at dusk and during the night for insects, spiders, slugs, worms, and other small creatures. When it is not hunting, it hides under stones and logs.

Mole salamanders

Mole salamanders live in North America in woodland and grassland areas. They live in burrows that they dig, or in holes abandoned by other small creatures. Some mole salamanders spend all winter in their burrows, but then they return to the ponds where they were born when it is time to breed.

Mole salamanders have smooth, shiny skin that can absorb oxygen.

If threatened, the fire salamander sprays a poisonous, milky fluid from glands along its back at the predator.

Hellbenders

Hellbenders, or giant salamanders, live in Japan, China, and North America. The two North American species grow up to 16 inches long, but their Japanese cousin grows up to 6 feet long. Hellbenders eat virtually any living thing that they find in the water, including **crayfish,** worms, and insects.

Hellbenders have wrinkly skin that oozes slime. The slime protects them from cuts and attacks from parasites.

ANIMAL FACT

In North America, hellbenders have many names, including devil dog and snot otter!

Beware dragons!

Turn to page 103 to find the sticker that completes this scene.

Some reptiles look like dragons and are even called dragons. They have scaly skin and long claws. Some have spikes all down their back.

Like many lizards, the Chinese water dragon can sense light through a small bump on the top of its head called a "third eye."

Komodo dragon

The Komodo dragon of Indonesia grows up to 10 feet long and is the largest species of lizard. It has a big appetite and can eat up to 80 percent of its body weight in one meal. It eats other reptiles, birds, monkeys, goats, deer, horses, and water buffalo.

Chinese water dragon

The Chinese water dragon lives in the rain forests of Southeast Asia. It often sits on branches overhanging water, and if startled, drops into the water and swims away. It can stay underwater for up to 30 minutes. The Chinese water dragon eats insects, small fish, rodents, and plants.

The Komodo dragon has long claws for catching hold of prey. It bites off chunks of meat with its teeth. Its saliva is filled with bacteria that help to kill its prey quickly.

Green iguana

The green iguana looks like a wingless dragon. It grows up to 6.5 feet long and has pointed scales along its back. Although it looks fierce, the green iguana is a herbivore, which means it eats only plants. It lives in Central and South America.

The green iguana's long fingers and claws enable it to climb trees and cling to branches.

ANIMAL FACT

Some people eat green iguanas. The dish is known as "bamboo chicken."

TRUE OR FALSE?

The Komodo dragon of Indonesia is the largest species of lizard; it grows up to 10 feet long.

Answer: True! (see page 48)

Create a scene

Use the stickers on page 99
to create your own amazing animal habitat!

Bizarre creatures

Turn to page 103 to find the sticker that completes this scene.

Common rain frogs get their name from their habit of calling during rainstorms.

Reptiles and amphibians have some amazing habits. One lizard, the common basilisk, can actually run across water.

Common basilisk

A young common basilisk can run about 30 to 60 feet across the surface of water without sinking. It does this when fleeing from predators. The common basilisk lives near streams and lakes in the rain forests of Central and South America. It eats insects, flowers, and other small creatures.

Common rain frogs

Tiny common rain frogs live in the rain forests of Central and South America, on some Caribbean islands, and in southern Africa. They lay their eggs in a cup of leaves or on a moist patch of the forest floor. The eggs hatch into frogs rather than tadpoles.

Webbing between the toes of the common basilisk helps it to run across water. On land, the webbing is rolled up.

Jackson's chameleon

The Jackson's chameleon comes from eastern Africa and has been introduced in Hawaii. The babies are born fully developed, rather than hatching from eggs.

The Jackson's chameleon is able to look in two directions at once. Males have three long horns.

QUESTION

What type of salamander sprays a poisonous, milky fluid when it feels threatened?

ANIMAL FACT

According to legend, the basilisk could kill things just by looking at them.

53

Answer: Fire salamander (see page 47)

Peculiar predators

Some reptiles and amphibians use a **lure** to attract prey. Others wait silently in hiding until prey passes, and then launch a sudden attack.

The death adder has a thick body and a short tail. It takes up to three years to reach adult size.

Alligator snapping turtle

The alligator snapping turtle lives in North America. It has a small, wormlike growth on its tongue that it wriggles to attract prey, especially fish. It also eats frogs, small snakes, and birds.

Death adders

Death adders live in Australia and New Guinea. They bury themselves in sand or **leaf litter,** so that only the head and tail are visible. To attract prey, the death adder dangles the tip of its tail, which looks like a worm. When a bird or mammal tries to grab the "worm," the death adder strikes and poisons its prey in a fraction of a second.

Turn to page 103 to find the sticker that completes this scene.

The alligator snapping turtle's jaws are strong enough to bite off a human finger.

Surinam horned frog

The Surinam horned frog lives in northern South America. It burrows itself into the ground and waits for prey. If a mouse, small lizard, or frog wanders past, the Surinam horned frog jumps out and grabs it.

ANIMAL FACT

Some Surinam horned frog tadpoles will eat each other after they hatch.

The Surinam horned frog is well camouflaged. The pattern on its skin makes it look like a leaf, so it is difficult to see on the forest floor.

Tricky tongues

The tongues of some reptiles are extremely long and sticky. Some have tongues that are V-shaped, and some have brightly colored tongues that they stick out to scare away predators.

Chameleons

When a chameleon sees prey, such as a grasshopper, cricket, or praying mantis, it aims its long, sticky tongue at the animal. As the tip of the chameleon's tongue hits the prey, it forms a cup shape that sticks to the creature and traps it. The chameleon then pulls the insect back into its mouth. Some large chameleons also eat other lizards and small birds.

With incredible speed, a Parson's chameleon shoots its tongue out at an insect on a twig. It can capture prey that is more than a body length away.

ANIMAL FACT

The sharp, venomous fangs of the diamondback rattlesnake can be more than 1 inch long.

The diamondback rattlesnake has a large, forked tongue that can "taste" the scent of prey on the air.

Diamondback rattlesnakes

The two species of diamondback rattlesnakes are North America's most poisonous snakes. They are aggressive, but warn predators of their presence by shaking the rattle at the end of their tail.

Blue-tongued skinks

When alarmed, the blue-tongued skink sticks out its tongue to scare away predators.

Blue-tongued skinks live in Australia and New Guinea. They sleep in leaf litter or fallen logs. During the day, they hunt for snails, slugs, insects, spiders, berries, flowers, **fungi,** and carrion. Although their teeth are not sharp, they can give a powerful bite.

Turn to page 103 to find the sticker that completes this scene.

Terrifying toads

Toads tend to travel farther from water than frogs, and their skin is often dry and bumpy, rather than smooth.

Star-fingered toads

Star-fingered toads, also called Surinam toads, live in the Amazon region of South America. When the female lays her eggs, they stick to her back with slime and gradually sink into her skin. About 12 to 20 weeks later, the babies push their way out of her skin and swim off.

The African clawed toad uses its sensitive fingers to find and catch prey. It uses its back feet to dig down into mud.

QUESTION

Which type of snake takes two to three years to reach adult size?

African clawed toad

The African clawed toad lives in water. It uses its claws to stir up mud to find insects to eat. If the toad's pond dries up, it buries itself in the mud and waits until it rains.

Answer: Death adder (see page 54)

Giant cane toad

The giant cane toad is from Central and South America. In 1935, it was introduced to Australia to control a beetle species that was damaging sugarcane crops. The toad bred quickly and is now a pest itself. Pets, humans, and the **native** animals that prey on frogs and toads all fall victim to its poison.

ANIMAL FACT

The largest giant cane toad was 9 inches—the size of a small dog!

The giant cane toad produces a poison from glands on each shoulder. If humans eat the poison, it can cause a heart attack.

Amazing adapters

To help them survive, some reptiles and amphibians have changed, or adapted, over time to new conditions. In hot, dry places they may live mainly underground, away from the heat of the sun, and come out only when it rains.

Tokay

The tokay is a **gecko.** It has developed special clingy toe pads for gripping. The pads are covered in tiny hairs. The ends of these hairs are split into many parts. These tiny hairs can stick to smooth surfaces. To release its grip, the tokay curls its toes. It lives in Southeast Asia, northeast India, Bangladesh, and New Guinea.

Water-storing frog

The water-storing frog lives in Australia. The frog stores water in large quantities in its **bladder** for use in dry periods. In hot conditions, it burrows into the mud and makes an underground hole, or cell. It may sleep there for several years, waiting for cooler, wetter weather to arrive.

The water-storing frog is seen only after heavy rain. When the male calls, it inflates its throat to make the sound louder.

Turn to page 103 to find the sticker that completes this scene.

ANIMAL FACT

Tokays are aggressive, and when they bite, they do not let go easily.

The tokay's soft, velvety skin is colored to help it blend in with tree bark.

Sirens

Sirens live in the southern United States in shallow pools and ditches that dry up in warm weather. When their pools dry up, sirens burrow into the mud and make a **cocoon** out of hardened slime and old skin. Large adults can survive this way without food for nearly two years.

Sirens have a horny, beaklike mouth and a pair of tiny front legs, but no back legs.

Slimy amphibians

Amphibians spend some of their time on land and some of their time in water. They are able to breathe through their skin, which they need to keep damp and slimy.

Olm

The olm lives in caves in parts of Europe. It is albino, which means it has no color at all in its skin. It is also blind, but it has good hearing and a strong sense of smell. The olm preys on crabs, snails, and bugs.

The sticky slime that slimy salamanders produce makes them a nasty meal for predators.

The olm is also called the humanfish because its skin is thought to resemble human skin.

Slimy salamanders

Slimy salamanders live in woodland in the United States. They do not have lungs, but take in air through their skin and the lining of their mouth. Slimy salamanders get their name from the slime that oozes from their skin. If you get it on your hands, it will stick like glue.

Gray foam-nest tree frog

The gray foam-nest tree frog lives mainly in southeast and south-central Africa. It lives in subtropical or tropical forests, grassland, shrubland, marshes, and even gardens. Foam-nest tree frogs save water in their bodies so that they can live in very dry places. They also produce slime that turns into a waterproof cocoon.

TRUE OR FALSE?

The tokay has soft, velvety skin that is colored to help it blend in with tree bark.

Pairs of gray foam-nest tree frogs make their foam nest on a branch overhanging rainwater pools. Tadpoles emerge from the eggs, and after about a week they drop from the foam into the water below.

ANIMAL FACT

The gray foam-nest tree frog turns almost white in hot weather. White reflects sunlight, so this helps keep the frog cool.

Answer: True! (see page 61)

CHAPTER 3:
BEASTLY BIRDS, BATS & BUGS

Freaky flyers

The world is full of amazing birds. They come in all shapes and sizes, from tiny wrens and hummingbirds to huge birds of prey. Birds are not the only animals that fly. Bats and insects fly, too. We will also look at some strange-looking bats and bugs.

Many birds carry food to their young in their stomach. They *regurgitate* the food for the young to eat.

While feeding from flowers, hummingbirds hover in midair. Most species do this by flapping their wings about 50 times per second.

All shapes of beaks

Some birds have developed special features and habits for survival. Ducks, for example, have paddle-shaped beaks to help them sieve food from the water. Hummingbirds have long, pointed beaks that they poke deep into flowers so they can drink the **nectar**.

Horrid habits

Birds have many habits that we might think of as unpleasant. These include feeding their young with regurgitated food. Some bats have horrid habits, too. The vampire bat drinks the blood of living creatures. Fruit bats, or flying foxes, like sweet fruit just like we do! They can be very large, with a wingspan of 5 feet. The fairyfly, a parasitic wasp, lays its eggs inside beetles' eggs.

TRUE OR FALSE?

A hummingbird flaps its wings about 50 times per second.

After they feed on fruit, fruit bats lick their claws clean.

Foul feeders

Birds such as vultures eat carrion. Turkey vultures sometimes regurgitate what they have eaten because the smell of rotting food puts off predators. Other birds regurgitate food to feed their young.

A baby gannet will tap its mother's beak to get her to regurgitate a meal of partially digested fish.

Gannets

Gannets are seabirds. They eat large amounts of fish such as pilchards, anchovies, and squid. Gannets often regurgitate the contents of their stomach if they are disturbed or alarmed.

The hoatzin cannot fly well. It spends a lot of time perching as it digests its meal, which makes it vulnerable to predators, such as monkeys.

Hoatzin

The hoatzin, or "stinky cowbird," is a South American cuckoo that smells of cow manure! It uses bacteria to ferment plant materials in the front part of its gut. This helps the bird digest its food. The smell is strong enough to put off predators.

Vultures

Vultures are scavengers—they eat the remains of dead animals that have been killed by predators, such as lions. Groups of vultures fly in circles above a dying animal, knowing that they will soon have a feast. Vultures have amazingly strong acid in their stomach to help them digest food. Some vultures can even digest bone.

Different species of vultures will feed on the same carcass at different times.

QUESTION

How long is a fruit bat's wingspan?

ANIMAL FACT

Most vultures have a bald head. Feathers would be difficult to keep clean, as the birds feed on carcasses.

Answer: 5 feet (see page 67)

Putrid pellets

Many larger birds, such as owls and birds of prey, hunt small animals and birds. They swallow their prey whole, but they cannot digest bones, feathers, or fur. These tough parts form pellets that the birds cough up and leave on the forest floor.

Peregrine falcon

The peregrine falcon hunts other birds. It flies over open ground and hedges to flush out its prey; then it swoops. Once it catches a bird, the falcon takes it to a "plucking post," such as a tree stump, and pulls out the bird's feathers before eating the rest.

Most large birds are beautiful and graceful creatures, but they are also aggressive predators.

ANIMAL FACT

A peregrine falcon punches its prey in midair with a clenched foot; then it turns to catch the prey as it falls.

Red-tailed hawk

The red-tailed hawk eats mice, squirrels, rabbits, and other birds. It watches for prey from a perch and then swoops down, sometimes flying low and chasing its **quarry** across the ground. The red-tailed hawk eats all of its prey, regurgitating the parts that it cannot digest in small pellets.

Turn to page 103 to find the sticker that completes this scene.

The red-tailed hawk has long, broad wings that help it soar through the air.

Owls

Part of an owl's stomach is called the **gizzard**. Here, the fur, bones, and other indigestible parts of its prey are squashed into a pellet. The stored pellet keeps the owl from feeding again, so the owl coughs up or regurgitates the pellet.

QUESTION

71

Dirty defenses

Birds need to defend themselves from the many predators that hunt them, including other birds. They have developed many different ways to do this, some of which are quite unpleasant!

Fulmars

If an intruder approaches a fulmar's nest, the fulmar makes a coughing noise and then spits oil at the attacker. Even fulmar chicks can do this. Very young chicks can spit small amounts of oil as soon as they leave the egg. By the time they are four days old, they can fire oil a distance of 12 inches. The chicks may have learned to do this because they are left alone in the nest for long periods while their parents hunt for food at sea.

Fulmar chicks use their spitting skills to defend themselves against feral cats, otters, skuas, crows, and gulls.

The fulmar lays its eggs on a grassy cliff edge. Once the chick is two weeks old, the adults leave in search of food.

Turn to page 103 to find the sticker that completes this scene.

Northern shoveler

The northern shoveler is a dabbling duck. It breeds in wetlands across much of North America, northern Europe, and Asia. If disturbed by a predator, the female shoveler sprays foul-smelling feces over her eggs to keep the predator from eating them.

Turn to page 103 to find the sticker that completes this scene.

The northern shoveler has a long, spoon-shaped bill for filter-feeding from the water. Its webbed feet help it swim.

Petrels

Petrels feed on crabs and fish. Giant petrels also eat **krill**, squid, dead seals, and dead penguins. Its stomach contains a thick, strong-smelling oil that it vomits at intruders. The oil makes feathers less waterproof, so it is dangerous for other birds.

ANIMAL FACT

The giant petrel is also known as a "stinker" due to the foul-smelling oil that it vomits at predators!

The petrel makes its nest in pebble-lined rock crevices.

Bully boys

The great skua makes harsh screams or barks when attacking intruders.

Birds can be vicious, both to other birds and to humans. Some birds attack other birds to kill and eat them. Some fight other birds to steal their food. Some attack to protect their chicks.

Great skua

The great skua is an aggressive bird with a wingspan of about 4.5 feet. Some people call it the "pirate of the seas." It attacks other birds and steals their prey, and kills and eats puffins and kittiwakes. Skuas also eat fish, lemmings, and the eggs and young of other birds.

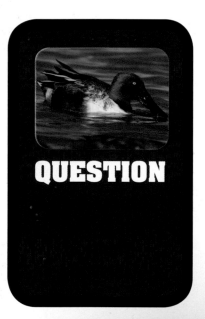

QUESTION

Male Australian magpies often attack humans and other birds, who they believe are a threat to their newly hatched chicks.

Magpies

Magpies are common birds often seen in the United Kingdom and Australia. They attack and eat the eggs and young of other birds, including chickens, and are often shot as **vermin** by farmers. The Australian magpie is a particularly aggressive species. A survey found that nine out of ten Australian men had been attacked by a magpie at some point in their lives!

Answer: Dabbling duck (see page 73)

Cuckoos

Many types of cuckoos have a bullying habit. The common cuckoo, for example, lays an egg in the nest of a smaller bird. The cuckoo's egg hatches first, and the small bird feeds the young cuckoo, which grows quickly. The cuckoo soon pushes the eggs or chicks of the smaller bird out of the nest.

The young cuckoo is much bigger than the adult foster bird.

Scavengers

Lots of birds find their food by scavenging. They may eat parts of carcasses left behind by other animals, or they may scavenge for food in trash dumps. Whichever method they choose, it can be a messy business.

The carrion crow's beak is thick and has a curved tip, ideal for picking up and carrying eggs.

Carrion crow

The carrion crow is a large, black bird that likes to sit on the top of isolated trees so it can spy on the surrounding countryside. It watches birds building their nests, and later attacks them, eating their eggs and young.

Crested caracara

The crested caracara, or Mexican eagle, is the national bird of Mexico. It prefers to eat carrion in the form of dead and rotting fish or roadkill. Sometimes it will attack brown pelicans and force them to disgorge the fish they have caught.

The male caracara often acts as a lookout, watching for danger from a perch near its nest, to protect its young.

QUESTION

Which bird is often seen in the United Kingdom and Australia?

Answer: Magpie (see page 74)

Marabou stork

The marabou stork is a large bird. Its wingspan can reach a huge 10.5 feet—the largest wingspan of any land bird, matched only by the Andean condor. The marabou stork scavenges on carrion and scraps. This may sound unpleasant, but it helps prevent the spread of disease.

The marabou stork's featherless head and neck are easy to keep clean as it feeds.

ANIMAL FACT

Marabou storks march in front of grass fires, snatching and eating the small animals that are fleeing.

Bizarre birds

Some birds look as if they have been put together using the various parts of other birds! From birds with strange beaks to birds with peculiar habits, there are some very bizarre birds in the world.

The secretary bird has long, skinny legs like a wading bird's and a body like an eagle's.

Secretary bird

The secretary bird lives in Africa. It appears on the coat of arms, or state emblem, of Sudan and South Africa. The bird has an unusual habit—it stamps hard on grassy tussocks with its feet. This scares any small lizards, mammals, birds, or grasshoppers that may be hiding there. As they run away, the secretary bird stamps on them to stun or squash them. Then it tears them apart using its hooked beak.

Sun bittern

The sun bittern is found in Central and South America. The adult birds perform a special "broken wing" trick to protect their nests. If a predator approaches, the sun bittern will drag one wing along the ground as if it is broken. The predator will follow the apparently injured bird, thinking it will be easy to catch.

When the sun bittern is scared, it raises its wings to show off two large eyespots. The "eyes" make the bird's body look like the head of a much bigger, scarier animal.

Spoonbills

Spoonbills wade through shallow water, swinging their open bill from side to side in the water. If any small fish, insects, or crustaceans touch the inside of the bill, the bird snaps it shut!

The spoonbill's beak has lots of detectors inside that feel vibrations. This enables the spoonbill to feed, even in murky water.

ANIMAL FACT

Spoonbill chicks sometimes die from starvation while their parents take too long looking for food.

Create a scene

Use the stickers on page 101
to create your own amazing animal habitat!

Big mouths

Some birds, such as pelicans, have a huge mouth that they use to snap up large prey. Other birds use their mouth to alarm predators. The bird may suddenly open its mouth wide to startle its enemy.

If frightened, a tawny frogmouth opens its beak wide and shows its yellow throat, hoping to scare away predators.

The toucan's large bill may put off predators, but it is not strong enough to be used as a weapon.

Tawny frogmouth

The tawny frogmouth lives in Australia. By day, it sits very still in trees and is difficult to spot. At night, it hunts for insects, which it may dig from the soil or catch while flying. The tawny frogmouth either beats its prey to death or swallows it whole.

Toucans

Toucans live in the rain forests of South America. They use their huge, colorful bills to pick fruit to eat. The length of the bill enables them to reach fruit on branches that are too small to take their weight. During the mating season, male and female toucans throw fruit at each other to attract a mate.

Pelicans

Pelicans are waterbirds found on many of the world's coastlines. A large pouch hangs under their beak. They eat fish, frogs, and crustaceans such as crab and shrimp. Sometimes they also eat smaller birds.

QUESTION

ANIMAL FACT

In medieval times, it was thought that mother pelicans fed their young with their own blood when food was scarce.

Pelicans expand their throat pouch to scoop prey out of the water. They drain off the water before swallowing the prey.

Answer: Pick up and carry eggs (see page 76)

83

Strange predators

Some birds have horrid hunting habits. They may beat or peck their prey to death, or even push it onto branches or rocks. One bird even drinks the blood of other birds.

Kookaburras have a loud call that sounds like hysterical laughter.

Vampire finch

The vampire finch lives on Wolf Island in the Galápagos. It feeds on blood, which it gets by pecking at the feet and wings of other birds. It also eats the eggs of seabirds called boobies.

A vampire finch feeds on the blood of a larger bird.

Kookaburras

Kookaburras live in Australia, New Zealand, and New Guinea. They mainly eat insects, worms, and crustaceans, but sometimes vary their diet with small snakes, mammals, frogs, and birds. They pounce on their prey from a perch, bashing large victims against a branch or the ground.

ANIMAL FACT

The vampire finch rolls the newly laid eggs of other birds against a rock to break them open. It then feeds on the contents.

European bee-eater

The European bee-eater is a **migratory** bird. It spends winter in warm places such as Africa, northwest India, and Sri Lanka, and the summer in Europe. It eats bees, wasps, and hornets. Before eating, the bee-eater hits the insect against its perch to knock out the stinger. In just one day, the European bee-eater eats as many as 250 bees.

European bee-eaters build burrowlike nests up to 5 feet long in banks or cliffs.

Stinky birds

Some birds are known for causing a real stink! Whether it is the birds themselves, their eggs, or the mess they make with their feces, the smell can be really awful.

Giant petrels

Northern and southern giant petrels lay stinky eggs. It is believed that the eggs' smell repels predators. Even after 100 years in museum collections, the eggshells still smell. The body of the southern giant petrel has a strong, musky smell, too. It feeds mainly on dead seals and penguins, as well as krill and squid.

Giant petrels regurgitate foul-smelling oil into their gravel nests to keep predators at a distance.

Turn to page 103 to find the sticker that completes this scene.

ANIMAL FACT

Starling guano is acidic and can damage buildings made of sandstone.

Hoopoes

Hoopoes are found in Europe, Asia, and Africa. The hoopoe makes a foul-smelling nest in a hole in a tree trunk or wall. It adds lots of feces to the nest to drive off predators. It also squirts feces at intruders.

The hoopoe eats insects and worms. It has a colorful crest that it raises when excited.

Starlings

Starlings are very common in Great Britain, where there are about 500,000 breeding pairs. The birds nest in spring, often in walls or attics. This can be a problem for homeowners, as the birds make lots of noise—and produce lots of guano, or feces. The guano is not only smelly, but it can also carry diseases.

In winter, thousands of migrant starlings arrive in Great Britain from eastern Europe. They stay there for the winter.

TRUE OR FALSE?

Answer: True! (see page 83)

Beastly bats

Many bats look very strange. Humans have made up stories about bats being evil because of the way they look. But they actually do a lot of good, eating large numbers of harmful insects.

The fringe-lipped bat gets its name from the growths on its lips and chin.

When roosting, the bat pulls up a fold of skin from its chin and hooks it over the top of its head, covering its ears.

Fringe-lipped bat

The fringe-lipped bat lives in Central and South America. It eats insects, other bats, and frogs. Just by listening to the frogs' mating calls, the bat can tell which frogs are poisonous and which are safe to eat.

Wrinkle-faced bat

The wrinkle-faced bat lives from southern Mexico to Venezuela. It has lots of hairless folds of skin on its face. The bat roosts in trees by day. After dusk, it eats fruit such as ripe bananas.

Spectral bat

The spectral bat is one of the largest bats in the world. It has a wingspan of up to 3 feet. It is found in southern Mexico, Ecuador, Peru, Brazil, Guyana, Surinam, and Trinidad. The spectral bat hunts at night for birds, small mammals, reptiles, frogs, large insects, and fruit—and even other bats! Both parents take care of the single baby that is born each year. The father bat often sleeps with both the mother and baby wrapped in its wings.

ANIMAL FACT

A spectral bat suddenly drops from a tree onto its prey as the prey passes below.

The spectral bat has long canine teeth. When it hunts, it drops onto its prey from above.

Poisonous flyers

Some birds have developed unusual protection against predators. They use poison in their feathers or skin to keep themselves safe from enemies.

Pitohuis

Pitohuis are songbirds from New Guinea. These birds have high levels of poison in their feathers and skin, and smaller amounts in their bodies. They eat a type of beetle that contains the poison. The poison may protect the birds from predators and parasites.

The pitohui may be brightly colored as a warning to predators that it is poisonous.

Quails are very small, only growing to about 7 inches high. They have many predators, including humans!

Quails

Some European and Eurasian quails are poisonous. People who have eaten quail in northern Algeria, southern France, Greece, northeastern Turkey, and Russia have been known to suffer vomiting, breathing problems, pain, and even paralysis.

Turn to page 103 to find the sticker that completes this scene.

Blue-capped ifrita

The blue-capped ifrita is a small, insect-eating bird found in New Guinea. It eats choresine beetles, which contain a poison. The poison is carried in the bird's blood and is laid down in its skin and feathers. This protects it from predators.

The feathers of the blue-capped ifrita are beautiful, but dangerous to touch.

Answer: Quail (see page 90)

QUESTION

ANIMAL FACT

The poison in the feathers of ifritas is the same poison as that found in poison dart frogs.

Foul flies

Flies can be very annoying, buzzing around our heads and landing on our food. If, however, you take a closer look, you will see that they are truly amazing flyers.

Snakeflies

There are about 200 different snakefly species. Snakeflies live in North America, Europe, and central Asia. They eat small prey, such as aphids and young caterpillars. The female lays eggs under bark. The eggs hatch into larvae that live under bark and in leaf litter.

An adult snakefly can lift its head high above the rest of its body, in a way that is similar to an attacking snake.

Blowflies include greenbottles and bluebottles. They are easily recognized by their metallic sheen.

Blowflies

Female blowflies lay eggs on meat or on the open wounds of injured animals such as sheep. A female blowfly can lay up to 2,000 eggs in her lifetime. Only eight hours after being laid, the eggs hatch into maggots, which feed on the meat.

ANIMAL FACT

Snakeflies are one of only two groups of insects that can run backward at full speed.

Robber flies

Robber flies are often found in dry, sandy places. They are aggressive hunters, preying on spiders, beetles, other flies, butterflies, bees, and other flying insects. A robber fly catches its prey in the air. It has a sharp point on its head that it uses to pierce the flesh of its prey. Then it injects saliva into the other creature. The saliva paralyzes the prey, so that the robber fly can suck out its juices.

A robber fly has a thick, bristly mustache that helps to protect its face from prey struggling to escape.

GLOSSARY

Adapt To change over many generations to suit the living conditions.

Altitude The height above sea level.

Amazon basin The part of South America drained by the Amazon River.

Amphibians Animals that can live both on land and in water, such as frogs, toads, newts, and salamanders.

Anacondas Large snakes that kill prey by crushing them with their body.

Antarctica The huge, cold continent around the South Pole. It is twice the size of Australia.

Appendage A body part such as an arm, leg, tail, or fin.

Bacteria Tiny organisms that can cause disease.

Biologists Scientists who study living things.

Bladder An organ found in the bodies of humans and other animals. It stores urine, which is produced by the kidneys.

Bubonic plague A serious, often fatal disease caused by bacteria. The disease may be passed from rats to humans by fleas that have lived on infected rats.

Carrion Dead or decaying flesh.

Cocoon A thin covering that some creatures make to enclose and protect themselves when they are not active.

Crayfish A freshwater creature that is similar to a lobster.

Cub The young of some animals such as bears, lions, and tigers.

Decibels A unit used to measure the power of sound. The higher the decibel number, the louder the sound.

Den A place wild animals make in which to sleep, rest, or hibernate. The animal may use a natural hollow in the ground, or it may build a den using leaves and branches.

Diabetes A disease that causes people to be unable to control the amount of glucose (a type of sugar) in their blood. Diabetes can be controlled with medicines such as insulin.

Dinosaurs Reptiles that became extinct millions of years ago. One of the best known dinosaurs was Tyrannosaurus rex, or T. rex.

Dry season In tropical climates, there can be dry and wet seasons. Rain falls heavily during the wet season; little or no rain falls during the dry season.

Endangered In danger of dying out or becoming extinct.

Extinction When the last of a species dies and no more individuals of the species exist.

Feces Waste matter that passes out from an animal's anus.

Fungi Plants without leaves or flowers, such as mushrooms and toadstools. They grow on other plants or decayed material.

Gecko Small reptiles that have toe pads that can stick to smooth surfaces.

Gills The organs that help water animals breathe. The gills take oxygen from the water.

Gizzard A thick-walled, muscular pouch in the lower stomach of many birds and reptiles that grinds food, often with the aid of ingested stones or grit.

Gland A part of an animal's body that secretes substances.

Habitat The natural surroundings of an animal.

Krill Small, shrimplike crustaceans eaten as food by certain fish and whales.

Larva The young of any invertebrate—an animal without a backbone, such as an insect. A larva is also the young of an animal that changes its form. A tadpole, for example, is the larva of a frog. Larvae hatch from eggs.

Leaf litter Dead plant material made from decaying leaves, twigs, and bark.

Lure Something such as an antenna or strange-shaped tail that looks like an insect or a worm. It is used by predators to attract prey that will want to eat the lure.

Mammals Warm-blooded animals with backbones and hair. They produce live young, not eggs. There are around 5,400 species of mammals, ranging from the huge blue whale to the tiny bumblebee bat.

Mange A skin disease in hairy animals such as dogs, caused by a tiny parasitic mite. Animals with mange often lose hair.

Mangrove swamp A marine (seawater) swamp found in tropical or subtropical places.

Migrate When animals move from one place to another, usually as the seasons change and food becomes scarce.

Native The place where a creature, plant, or person originally comes from or was born.

Nectar A sweet liquid produced by a plant, which attracts the insects or birds that pollinate the flower.

Northern Hemisphere The half of the earth between the North Pole and the equator.

Parasites Plants or animals that live by feeding on other living things. A tapeworm is a parasite that lives inside other animals and feeds on them.

Predator A creature that hunts and kills other animals for food.

Prey An animal that is hunted by another animal.

Quarry An excavation or pit, usually open to the air, from which building materials are obtained.

Regurgitate To bring up undigested food or liquids.

Rodents A group of animals that includes rats, mice, voles, squirrels, and shrews.

Roundworms Any nematode (a type of worm with a rounded body) that lives in the intestines of humans and other mammals.

Rump The backside or buttocks of a large animal.

Saliva The liquid that forms in the mouth.

Scavenge To hunt for and eat dead animals or carrion. Vultures and hyenas are scavengers. They feed on the bodies of animals that have been killed by predators.

Secrete To release liquid, especially from glands in the body.

GLOSSARY

Sewers Underground pipes and tunnels that carry away sewage from toilets and wastewater from households.

Snout The projecting nose and mouth of an animal.

Species A group of animals with similar characteristics that can breed with each other.

Spur A sharp, bony spike on the back of an animal's leg.

Suction The act of sucking. Some animals have suction cups on their feet or legs that help them grip their prey or steep, slippery surfaces.

Tadpoles The newly hatched young of creatures such as frogs, toads, and newts.

Tapeworms Long, parasitic flatworms that live in the intestines of animals such as pigs, dogs, and humans.

Tapir A creature with a heavy body and short legs, similar in shape to a pig. It is related to the horse and the rhinoceros.

Termite mound Termites construct a nest about 3 feet below the ground. Above the nest, they pile up the earth into huge mounds full of tunnels, where they live.

Territory The area of land that an animal defends against other animals of the same species. Some animals mark the boundary of their territory with scent, and they hunt within that area.

Toxin A poisonous substance, especially one formed in the body.

Typhus A serious infectious disease caused by bacteria passed on by lice and fleas. It causes headaches, fever, and reddish spots all over the body; it can be fatal.

Venom The poison used by some mammals, snakes, and spiders to paralyze or kill their prey.

Vermin Small animals or insects that are harmful and are often difficult to control.

Worming When an animal is wormed, it is given a medicine that kills parasitic worms living in the intestines.

Create-a-scene stickers

Create-a-scene stickers

Create-a-scene stickers

101

Bonus stickers

Bonus stickers

Bonus stickers

III

Bonus stickers

Question

Ringing True

Q: How can a scientist tell how old a crocodile is?

A: Like trees, crocodiles have growth rings on their scales.

Question

True or False:

There are almost 3,000 species of snakes.

Turn card over for answer.

Joke

Q: What did one flea say to the other flea?

A: Should we walk or take the dog?

Puzzle

Rearrange the letters to spell the name of a freaky creature. Then decide if the creature is a fish or an insect!

HVRILSEFSI

Turn card over for answer.

Question

Multiple Choice

Which animal is related to the okapi?

A. Aye-aye
B. Giraffe
C. Numbat
D. Solenodon

Turn card over for answer.

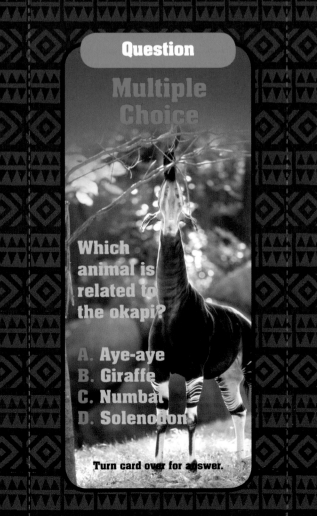

Fun Fact

What's in a name?

The insects known as harvestmen are sometimes called "daddy longlegs" due to their tiny bodies and lengthy limbs.

Joke

Q: What's smaller than an ant's mouth?

A: An ant's dinner!

Answer

True!
There are many different types of snakes, ranging from small garter snakes to gigantic boas and pythons.

Fun Fact

Keeping Their Cool
After a period of activity, such as chasing prey, crocodiles and alligators tend to overheat. To cool down, they rest in shade or lie in water.

Not-so-fun Fact

Puny Pests

Fleas are tiny vampires of the insect world, feeding on warm blood. Fleas attack dogs, cats, pigs, and humans.

Answer

B. Giraffe

Answer

SILVERFISH

The silverfish is an insect that has existed for more than 300 million years!

Match It Up

Match each slimy creature to its habitat.

A. Salamander
B. Jellyfish
C. Gray foam-nest tree frog
D. Sludge worm

1. The ocean
2. A tropical rain forest
3. A pond
4. Woodlands

Turn card over for answers.

Fun Fact

Warming Up

Crocodiles have structures in their skin that trap heat to keep their cold-blooded bodies warm.

Fun Fact!

Deadly Bait

Some species of anglerfish use a glow-in-the-dark lure attached to their head to attract food. Since there is no light in the deep ocean, curious fish swim toward the glowing lure before becoming the anglerfish's next meal!

Game

What Am I?

I have a beak like a bird, spines like a hedgehog, eggs like a reptile, the pouch of a marsupial, and the life span of an elephant.

Turn card over for answer.

Question

True or False?

A diamondback rattlesnake has reserve fangs to replace any that break off when it bites.

Turn card over for answer.

Fun Fact

Old Timers

Alligator snapping turtles can live up to 150 years!

Word Scramble

Use the letters below to spell out a word that describes animals with a hard outer shell, such as crabs and lobsters.

N C T S U R E C A A

Answer: Crustacean

Enough Is Enough!

A leech can suck out a host's blood for 30 minutes to an hour, ingesting five times its body weight before having to let go!

A-4
Salamanders are found in woodlands.

B-1
Jellyfish live in the ocean.

C-2
Gray foam-nest tree frogs live in Africa's rain forests.

D-3
Sludge worms live at the bottom of ponds.

Q:

What is a snake's favorite subject?

A:

Hisssssstory!

True!

Rattlesnake fangs are continuously lost and replaced every six to ten weeks. If a rattlesnake breaks a fang as a result of biting, it's simply replaced with the next available fang.

I'm an echidna!

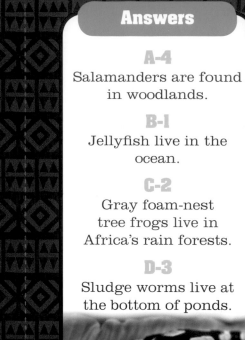

Poisonous Birds

Birds such as the pitohui and blue-capped ifrita have poison in their feathers. How do the birds become poisonous?

Turn card over for answer.

True or False?

Gila monsters are known for having the cleanest mouths of any reptile.

Turn card over for answer.

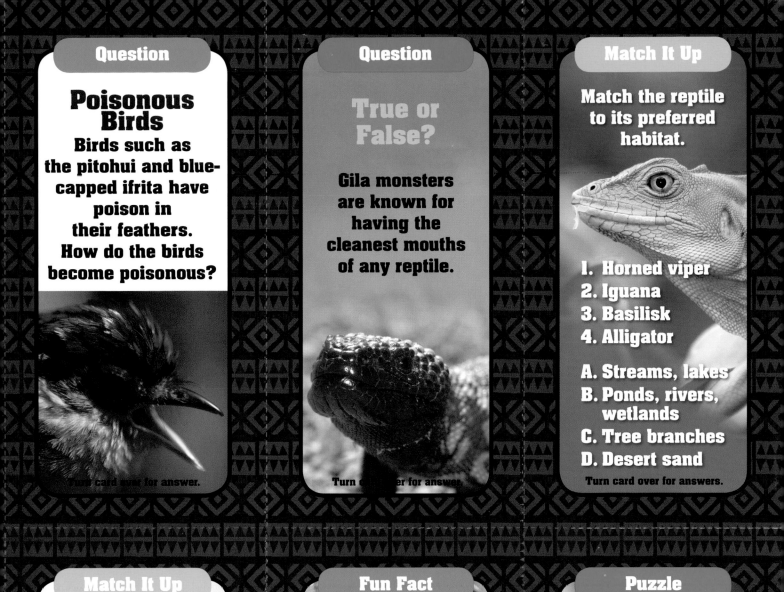

Match the reptile to its preferred habitat.

1. Horned viper
2. Iguana
3. Basilisk
4. Alligator

A. Streams, lakes
B. Ponds, rivers, wetlands
C. Tree branches
D. Desert sand

Turn card over for answers.

Hunter and Hunted

Match up the birds with the food they like to eat.

1. Peregrine falcon
2. Pelican
3. Hoopoe

A. Fish, shrimp, frogs
B. Insects, worms
C. Other birds

Turn card over for answers.

Bats

There are approximately 1,100 bat species worldwide. About 70 percent eat insects, while the rest are frugivores, or fruit eaters!

Word Scramble

Unscramble the letters below to spell the name of a noisy Australian bird.

BORAKUKORA

Turn card over for answer.

Answers

1-D
Horned vipers live in the African desert.

2-C
Iguanas live in trees in Central and South America.

3-A
Basilisks live near streams and lakes.

4-B
Alligators call ponds, rivers, and wetlands home.

Answer

False!
The Gila monster's mouth is full of toxic saliva that it uses to poison its prey. Four potentially lethal poisons have been found in Gila monster venom.

Answer

Both the pitohuis and blue-capped ifrita eat poisonous insects. The poison is carried through the birds' blood to its skin and feathers.

Answer

Kookaburra
Olly the kookaburra, along with Millie the echidna and Syd the platypus, was one of the three mascots chosen for the 2000 summer Olympics in Sydney, Australia.

Game

Word Challenge

How many words can you make from the letters of ECHOLOCATION?

Echolocation is the process by which bats emit high-pitched sounds while listening to their echoes in order to locate prey and nearby objects.

Answers

1-C
Peregrine falcons prefer the meat of other birds!

2-A
Pelicans prefer fish, shrimp, frogs, and other water creatures.

3-B
Hoopoes have long beaks to catch insects and worms, their favorite foods.

Fun Fact

The Mind's Eye

The tarsier's eyeballs are enormous—each is approximately 16 millimeters in diameter. Each eye is as large as its entire brain!

Question

Multiple Choice

Reptiles and amphibians take on the temperature of their surroundings. Their bodies are hot or cold depending on their environment.

They are:
A. Warm-blooded
B. Green-blooded
C. Cold-blooded
D. Red-blooded

Turn card over for answer.

Fun Fact

What is a gizzard?

The gizzard is a special organ found in the digestive tracts of some animals, such as birds, reptiles, and earthworms. Its thick, muscular walls help grind up food for easy digestion.

Game

Meat Eaters

Which three animals prefer to eat meat?

Numbat
Star-nosed mole
Tasmanian devil
Echidna
Wolf
Aye-aye
Hyena

Turn card over for answers.

Game

What animal looks like a masked bandit?

Answer: Raccoon

Match It Up

Match the question with the correct answer.

A. How many teeth does an alligator have?

B. How many pounds does a crocodile weigh?

C. How many hours can a crocodile remain underwater?

D. How many years do alligators live?

1. Up to 5
2. About 50
3. Up to 1,100
4. 74 to 80

Turn card over for answers.

"Wise" Owls

The ancient Greeks associated the owl with Athena, goddess of wisdom and the arts. Thanks to this, the owl has enjoyed the reputation of being a smart, knowledgeable bird!

C.
Unlike warm-blooded mammals, reptiles and amphibians are cold-blooded.

Having a Ball

Pangolins have the ability to curl up into a ball when threatened, and it takes considerable force to unroll them. The cutting action of their scales will inflict serious wounds to anything inserted between them!

A. 4
B. 3
C. 1
D. 2

Alligators in the wild live to be between 35 and 50 years old, but alligators in captivity can live up to 80 years!

Q: What kind of shoes do frogs wear?

A: Open-toad sandals!

The Tasmanian devil, wolf, and hyena are meat eaters.